THE GOD'S HUSTLER

HUSTLER

LIBERTY KINGSDALE

First edition: June 2018
10 9 8 7 6 5 4 3 2 1
Mwariwangu, Liberty
The God's Hustler/
Liberty Mwariwangu.—1st ed.
1. Success—Religious aspects—Christianity. 2. Christian life.
3. Experience I. Title

Dedicated to my dear wife Alpha, thank you so much for your support and patience during the course of writing this book. It's not easy to be an author's wife.

My biological father, Obert, you are the biggest hustler I know, it is your hustle that raised me to become the man I am. I am not ashamed to be your son.

My mother, Loina. Your prayers and unconditional love makes anything possible. Don't get tired in well doing.

My late brother Michael, some of the invaluable principles you taught me are canonised in this book. You remain my hero even from your grave!

CONTENTS

PART I: **INTRODUCTION**

I HAD been stuck for hours in my study in the process of writing my other book different from this one when I started feeling tired and dizzy.

I am usually a victim of such numbness, especially when I commit to long hours of mental concentration on writing or reading, but something was more unusual this sunny afternoon, my head felt much lighter than on other days, and I felt an emptiness in my stomach despite the heavy brunch I had taken an hour earlier.

This is when I ventured out of my nest for recess. I started trotting —

the dusty streets of my neighbour-hood to refresh for one hour before resuming crafting my new title.

I was singing to myself along the way, when I came across a bunch of young folks, possibly in their twenties, who were standing under a tree shade on the sidewalk.

They were evidently arguing on something which I knew would eventually erupt into a fight if not intercepted.

This sight provoked me and made the inspirational speaker in me to click into his element. I felt driven to spoon out a motivational buffet

to stir these young hearts to do something worth with their time other
than unproductive social hangouts.

I did so for a good half an hour and
the gang started disintegrating. Each
went his way scratching his brow,
evidence to me that I had provoked
them to the core.

As they went, I saw a determination
in them to start a new life of produc-
tivity and progress.

At this time, my one-hour recess
was nearing exhaustion then I started pacing homeward. It is along the
path to my crib that I conceived
'The God's Hustler' title.

In the distant, I saw three remarkable men approaching my vantage, and as they neared, I felt a death-thawing breeze baptising my body into the coolness of the day.

The men were handsome and well-built, however, the one in the middle was head and shoulders above the rest and the grace that accompanied them sent the most intriguing sensation to my melanin skin.

On the path, the two on the sides halted as the one in the middle continued towards me. I got engulfed into a super-love moment when he pulled out his hand to greet me. He prophesied about a shift coming into the marketplace and afterward went personal. "You're being called to disciple the marketplace, to produce principals in this sphere for the Lord Jesus Christ."

That made me reflect on my inadequacies, like experience, knowledge, grooming and expertise in the world of business. I went breathless for a moment at such a commissioning.

The man discerned my doubts and reminded me about a lesson from my college mentor. He said: "Unlike men who call the qualified, God qualifies those he calls."
His graceful words rammed a force of confidence in my heart searing

an assurance that I could ace this assignment as long I was operating in His grace.

The man continued his charge: "Write down the inspiration and experiences you shall receive and share them with the world. The wisdom you shall spit on those pages shall be critical to the birthing of titans in the marketplace."

At this juncture, a realisation that God is the creator of all and is equally concerned with the marketplace as he is in church business oozed and billowed from my soul. That challenged my faith, but I was already soaring on this new found understanding; if we are God's —

children, then He must be interested in everything that touches our lives, spiritual, physical, social and economical.

I was delirious with regards to my new-found assignment. I felt ecstatic, humbled and honoured all at the same time.

The book I was working on had been intercepted and thus shelved for a little while to follow the trail of my new calling.

The further I followed the trail, the deeper I grooved myself into extra-terrestrial experiences which have a strong lean on helping God's people to dominate in life —

and the marketplace. 'The God's Hustler' is brewed from instruction, not mere inspiration. I scribed it from the celestial chambers of the Almighty, which is why I am fully persuaded that applying the principles herein, will bring great nourishment.

This chronicle is an antidote to all stagnation, poverty, mediocrity and regression. It is a kind of steroid that will stir you to outdo yourself.

To obtain the best from this canon, do not rush to complete reading it in one goal. The articles herein are independent from each other, hence it is good to read one article every morning before you venture into —

your daily business. Internalise the message through meditation and regard my experiences herein as your own.

In this regard, you will arm yourself with the right arsenal capable of altering the landscape of your business life. You are super-advantaged to be holding this book, find meaning from reading it!

It is a marketplace devotional distilled to compel the best out of you, and those around you. 'The God's Hustler' is a prerequisite for political leaders, business leaders, church leaders, community leaders, parents and young adults that are passionate in championing their cause in the marketplace and impart the same into others.

CHAPTER 1: **TODAY I SHINE**

TODAY, I shine in my heritage, I choose to influence my surroundings and the people around me positively, because my greatness will be seen by the positive virtues I impart into others.

I give up a selfish and meager life as I embrace my goodly heritage where lines fall for me in pleasant places.
I embrace a culture of giving, a language of love and an attitude of motivation.

I will not withhold my words of encouragement to the bowels that hunger for them. I will articulate words that are sweet to the ear's palate, but compelling enough to

wed my mates to Action, an ancestor of all Greatness.

I will take the initiative to simplify
our organisation's mission and I will
make it my daily routine to verbalise
it to them, a credo that will give them
tenacity of the soul that refuses to call
it a day before accomplishing their
daily tasks and objectives.

Today, I take an oath to value re-
lationships, and thus, I will take the
initiative to praise and appreciate
my fellow workmates, holding in
high esteem their good intentions
and helping them to vigorously act
on them in order to produce grand
results that will make my company
an Eden, a paradise that flourishes in

oneness, a quality that in the end, translates into progress and profits.

Daily, I will add to my quiver loyal relations as I put away the foul language that alienates others. If I overstep my bounds and offend someone, I will sincerely apologise without wasting time, and thus conceal revenge and flush the venom of vendetta.

I will nurture long-yielding relations with my clients, treating each potential customer as king and ruthlessly shutting the doors of escape once I lure them into my chambers.

Far be it from me to forget that my next meal is dependent on them.

I will make deliberate efforts to recognise what is important to them and dine with them on their milestones.

Even when they heed the call of the grave, I will inherit their families as I continue my tireless hustle for the next customer.

The people I work with will not assume anymore that I am on a mission of progress and profit, through my words and actions they will see and know it.

I will take the instruction of a wise ancient who taught: "Do Business till I come." I will encourage all of them to combine efforts and work as a team; my words will transform them into a forceful fist that breaks every wall of corporate intimidation.

I will be the soul of my company, and I will be the spring of inspiration were their thirsty souls come to drink. I am created in God's image, and thus I am a possessor of answers. I will grant solutions to every challenge that crosses my path.

I will bury selfishness in another planet, and I will make it impossible to exhume it. I will incorporate others in my quest for greatness, and will spruce-up my shine. Like a star, I will shimmer my best in brightening the earth.

I will not be intimidated by rank or office anymore; I will deal with all people primarily as humans. As long they have a soul, they have hunger to fill-up the mental-gut with inspiration.

Motivation is like bathing, you need it every day. The only credential required from me to inspire others is my very presence on this planet.

I will be relentless in undertaking projects. I will liken myself to an ant who builds castles, one grain at a time. I will be limitless like an eagle, who glides rough tempests to altitudes unfathomable. I will be like a vine, so lean that it needs —

the support of pillars to stand, but producing wine that staggers those who drink of it.

Like a reed, I will swing-back at every attempt the wrath of the flood overpowers me, and like a weed, I emerge again and again, refusing to recognise competition, seeking to annihilate me.

Today, I choose to shine in my heritage; I choose to influence my surroundings and the people around me positively.

CHAPTER 2: **I'M AN OAK**

IN THE wild, the Oak is idolised as the goddess of the jungle; the stupendous strength of her lumber compels attention of furniture lovers from around the globe.

She attracts a fortune for her exploiters who amass great wealth by putting high price-tags on her produce, afforded only by the deep pocketed.

By her splendor, citizens of the world build majestic and awe–striking handiwork. They construct beauteous cribs, lining them with her veins throughout. It is a noble thing to appreciate that her heroic muscle didn't reach full-maturity in a day. She earned this precious laurel through persistence.

Today, I must adopt the character of the Oak to make it in this economic jungle. Many ventured unprepared, and didn't last for long.

I will be persistent in exerting myself towards obtaining my vision — the eye of the mind. It sees places yonder, the canyons and the mountains of adversity, stirring devotion within the bowels of the soul in which a yearning to dwell such lands is fuelled and ultimately birthing commitment, a virtue that bulldozes through the hurdles pitched in her path, thwarting to obscurity those that resist her and elements beyond the unknown ravines.

Today, I must adopt the character of the Oak, if I am to make it in this economic jungle.

In a vision by night, I beheld a tiny grain so little as the head of a pin, swaying back and forth in the wind and lost in the dust of the gust. I struggled as my soul lingered for the sight of it amidst the blizzard of the thick dust.

When the wind relented, a voice thundered deafeningly to my ears: "Son of man, Lo and behold that grain." I scampered towards it and as I mounted the rock on which it sat, accidentally, I kicked it and there it fell into a cleft so deep and narrow that only a miracle could rescue it.

My heart bled for this little grain as tears flooded my eyes before the voice that spoke to me boomed again:

"Today you must adopt the character of the Oak, if you are to make it in this economic jungle!"

On the wings of time, the sun fled, kissing the western horizons before it went deep into the entrails of her womb, and behold, it was night. Around the third watch, the eastern wind whistled for frost and dew then dawn finally arrived with the morning. The eastern horizon spat the orange ball from her innards, and in a little while, the sun shone, casting her rays into the cleft.

The darkness therein leapt like a ram, and went to hide. Clearly in the daylight, I saw a little, tender yellow-leafed plant, emerging from the soil down below.

Today, I must adopt the character of the Oak if I am to make it in this economic jungle.

As days expired into nights, the mornings also emerged into days as the once little plant transformed by each heartbeat. It took root and claimed height. With the height it thickened, firming its stature. A day finally arrived when the cleft threatened the further growth of the tree.

The Oak had claimed the entire space within this crevice, but a flaming desire within her to become humongous wouldn't relent. She couldn't take no for an answer.

Today, I must adopt the character of the Oak if I am to make it in this economic jungle.

As I stood there, I heard a noise and a shaking. Cracks veined across the parched soil, rifting the rocks as this Titan tussled for a greater room.

The vision to become palace-worth prompted this Oak to despise her present limitations.

She found strength and guile within herself to part the rocks that could have strangled her growth, but in the process getting more toughened by the scars she suffered.

Today, I must adopt the character of the Oak if I am to make it in this economic jungle.

CHAPTER 3: **THINK VICTORY**

TODAY, I am rising up to victory and I shall accomplish with great success the dreams I have for so long laid in my mind.

I will do business in an unusual manner, for unusual results cannot be achieved through usual methods. The unusual calls for the unusual as the deep calls for the deep.

I will strengthen my hustle as I embark on my business hunt of today and I will surely come back to my nest with nothing but the emblems of Victory. Doubtlessly, I will add people, peace, money and opportunities to my treasury.

Today, I think Victory, for as a man thinks in his heart, so is he!

I will reap peace because I will administer my hustle in purity, taking nothing that promotes decadence or graft. I will pocket money because I will use my thinking faculties — a niche of the mind that most fools shun. Ultimately, I will come home with opportunities, the assurance of future prosperity.

Today, I think Victory, for as a man thinks in his heart, so is he!

Today, I conceal the lion in me behind a smile, for a smile is the magnet that pulls gold from peoples' purses. It has a miraculous effect that turns potentials into clients, be-fore converting them into money.

I will be aggressive in spirit, har-bouring an unweaning resolve nev-er to lose track of the prey I set mine eyes on. Yet, I will show tenderness and intense love, for people have a weakness — they gravitate towards love hot spots.

Today, I think Victory, for as a man thinks in his heart, so is he!

Today, I employ persuasive meth-ods to sell genuine products and services for this is the only security I will use to secure my clients from competitors. Gullible methods will only give instant gratification, with no lasting wealth. I will build trust with my contacts by supplying them the waters from my cistern, the waters that no other person will ever supply, such that when they thirst, they will come to buy from me again and again.

I will make myself likable to my clients and intoxicate them with so much love that they won't dread paying me commercial value for the goods and services I sell. I understand that people buy into the seller before paying for the merchandise.

Today, I think Victory, for as a man thinks in his heart, so is he!

CHAPTER 4: **PLEDGE YOURSELF**

TODAY, I pledge myself to the Lord of the marketplace for He delights in the prosperity of his servant.

Today, marks the beginning of the best things of my life, good and better now belong to yesterday. In the past I sowed good and better, no wonder I reaped a mediocre harvest that I consumed in tears with no surety of succeeding in the future, but today, I will give my best shot in all I do.

It is the order of the universe to give lemons to the one who sows a lemon tree and apples to the farmer of apple trees.

In my ventures of today, I will issue out my best thoughts and exert my youthful vigour towards my daily hustle, for success comes with effort. The Lord of the marketplace honours the smart and diligent, they will stand before kings and never will they serve ordinary men.

One Saturday afternoon, I went for a stroll and later decided to nap in the park. I folded myself into the available chair to watch a blissful sight of swallows that skated the mild wind–terrain.

In a moment, my surroundings altered and it felt like the sun had set on me. I sat there frozen with no command nor control over my –

body as the drama of the ancients played before me.

There was a man whose name was Raphael, who in his daily hustle to lead a meaningful life, followed a whisper in his heart, he believed an inner voice that spoke so loud to his entire being.

"I will make you into a great nation and I will bless you; I will make your name great and you will be a blessing"

He went every place this whisper led him to, and did what it commanded. He later realised that the Lord of the marketplace had spoken to him through his thoughts.

In the end, Raphael became very wealthy in livestock and silver and gold.

As this unusual sight faded away, it left a resolve drumming my heart. A resolve to start a new culture of seeking His counsel every dawn, and ask for his blessing upon my hustle, for He rewards loyalty and delights in the prosperity of his servant.

Seeing the need that had arisen in his country, Hezik considered the vastness of his wealth, the Lord of the marketplace had given him. He interceded for the ailing in his nation, but a compelling thought continued to churn his bowels:

"worship without sacrifice is mean-ingless."

From that moment, he objected the thought of leaving his purse behind whenever he consulted the Lord of the marketplace.

One day, in the heat of a merciless pestilence that forced many to retire to the graveyard, Hezik scouted for a piece of land that was conducive, so he could offer sacrifices of peace on it.

It happened that this most suitable ground belonged to his palace ser-vant Larush. Larush offered to free-ly give-up his land plus all the re-quired sacrifices for this cause, but

Hezik withstood him. He said, I will not offer that which cost me nothing and thus he bought this land for a fee and thawed the anguish that had ravished his land.

A cool breeze blew by, waking me up, then a distinct whisper followed, searing an imprint on my mind and a rigorous instruction to always honour Him with a part of my gold when I am done with my hustle for the day.

It was now past six in the evening when I rose up from the garden chair to head home with a bouquet of lessons key to my future prosperity;

- Seek His counsel every morning
- Ask for His blessing upon my hustle
- Honour Him with a part of my gold after every hustle

CHAPTER 5: **LASTING LEGACY**

AS I FEASTED the comfort of my bed, I aimlessly folded my arms behind my head with my fingers knitted together behind my occiput.

Suddenly, the thoughts of how I came into existence leached into my mind, and in no time, those thoughts became more real than my daily hustle in the marketplace — more real than life itself.

I could feel them beyond the wildest feeling, it was as if my entire mental gadgetry had transformed into one, so I could grasp what was to follow. In the meanwhile, an aggressive affirmation incessantly chimed in my soul: "I am wired to create a lasting legacy in the marketplace!"

A sweet sensation filled the room, ushered by an overwhelming aura, it would be an understatement to say all the perfume in the world would make up for that life-inspiring aroma.

I watched as everything around turned into gold, followed by a soul-pricking symphony that serenaded the room.

The choir caroled lyrics that merged with those that rang in my head:

"You are made to create a lasting legacy in the marketplace!"

Like an early morning-breeze, the Lord of the marketplace entered the room adorned in perfect-white raiment that harmonised with the golden sash around his waist. He alighted from his fiery-golden chariot then paced a few steps towards my location.

His fire-spitting eyes radiated authority as he pulled his right hand from the robe's wide mouthed sleeve. The wonder-hand was beautifully clad in a golden bracelet and a golden ring that was dotted with twelve precious stones, a perfect artwork from beyond our world.

Before he handed me the lit-
tle-art-crafted box which he held
in his marvelous hand, he rumbled:

"You were created for the marketplace, so create a lasting legacy in
it!"

With his voice that sounded like
a million voices combined, he
charged: "Every person has a pen to
write their name with in the cor-
ridors of Greatness, but only a few
are willing to hustle for the ink.

Press your mind to think and
compel your body to act on the
good thoughts, that way, you distill
your own ink to supremacy.

Life is a hustle of the minds, the one with the smartest ideas, prospers the most."

I fell face down at his power-sizzling words, my mental capacities couldn't comprehend at first the depth and the height of this truthful and thought provoking declaration.

I lay prostrate for some time, but like raindrops through a leaking roof, the charging whisper continued to plague my conscience;

I am wired to create a lasting legacy in the marketplace!

A sharp jab pierced my side, and then, I rolled over because of the pain, shrills of empowerment entered me as this Master of commerce commanded: "Be strong and unseal this golden case!"

As I acted on his command, the next thing I saw was a wagon of present and past history-makers. The folks that paraded our earth, leaving indelible footprints in the world of business.

The wagon railed into history, distancing itself from my vantage. It transformed into a scroll which then suspended in the air. The graceful Master plucked it as if from a tree and handed it over to me. I fell full length when I received it because I had not lifted an object this heavy ever since I slid from my-mother's womb. With a voice that thundered like a thousand torrents, He belched: "Son of man, chew this scroll."

I motioned my mouth towards it like a hungry cow that has found fresh pasture. It tasted sweet like a confection to my tongue, sweet-er than the sugars of Hippo Valley and Triangle combined, however, I couldn't settle when it entered my entrails.

Vibrations and pulls that made me feel replicated in numerous ways made me believe that I could win in anything. Then with a voice that sounded like a blast from ten-thousand nostrils, he snorted:

"You are born for the hustle, go and perpetuate a lasting legacy in the marketplace!"

CHAPTER 6: **MERGING MINDS**

THE PARADOX that sexual intimacy reproduces another life totally independent from the ones involved in its creation is a wonder in itself.

It means that no man has the ability to reproduce unless he collaborates with a woman who provides the womb which nurtures the deposited seed internally until delivery.

Even when the child is born, elders say, it takes a village to raise one. Such is life, it is so diverse and cannot be defined by words alone. It only multiplies when we merge efforts with minds and abilities different from ours.

Today, I collaborate with people gifted differently from me for life is like a mathematical problem, figures are not sufficient to make it understandable, we can only get solutions to mathematical problems when we collaborate figures with words.

I will not show foolishness through discriminating people by race, colour, profession, or level of education, for the mind is neither black nor white. The sun collaborates with the moon to give light at night.

Today, I merge with minds and abilities different from me for I can only multiply through others!

Today, I will fly with birds of a different feather for the world to see my distinctness.

The marketplace is like a football pitch and my hustle is the game, hence I will choose a different of kind of play that merges well with my fellow teammates in order to produce impressive results.

Stars don't shine their best by competing with the sun, they recognise that the sun is the greatest of all the stars, and they capitalise on her powerful rays to score their best during the night when the sun retires to her nest.

Today, I merge with minds and abilities different from me for I can only shine my best through others!

I will have opponents not enemies, for off-pitch, I can relate with them hence granting self an opportunity to learn their intentions and plans, helping me to sail on informed progressive patterns.

Having an opponent provides ample ground for breeding healthy competition — necessary space to demonstrate the best of my skills.

An enemy is a creature of negative perception. Depending on your vantage point, you will discover that your enemy is gold to some.

Opposition is necessary, like an arrow in the bow of a hunter, it propels us into rain-forests of greater and wider possibilities.

Today, I create opponents not enemies for both are creatures of perception.

Opponents give opportunities to learn when enemies zap my strength, relegating me to idleness.

I am the light of the world, and for that reason, I will not curse darkness, I will simply increase my shine by teaming up with others. Together, we will emit the brightest light and, by its radiation, convert the darkest nights-into brightest days. We will be the beacon that beams signals for the thirsty and parched souls in the marketplace. I will make my nights profitable by capitalising on their darkness, for this is the best way to relate with the night.

Today, I will not curse the darkness for it is an opportunity for me to shine!

Strength in isolation is weakness and weakness in another's company is strength. Weakness is a simple indication of what I don't have, telling me to team up with the people who are stronger in that area. No one subject in life can make me a master of everything, hence I have need to belong to a team. The old saint was right when he chronicled: "We know in part and we prophesy in part", I will not practice selfishness as if I have monopoly over knowledge.

Today, I merge with minds and abilities different from me for only then can my knowledge reach perfection!

I would rather achieve small with a team than achieving greater things single-handedly, for achieving greatness single-handedly is a myth, there is always the contribution of someone in the background. Achievements are magnified when won with a team, for one can only chase a thousand, but two put ten thousand to flight. I will celebrate going home with a leg of an elephant than the full body of an ant.

Teams have the magic of bringing surplus to households. As the baker collaborates with an oven to ripen his bread, I also will take advantage of people gifted differently to ripen my bread of prosperity.

Today, I will belong to a team for only then can my small strength create surplus for me and my household!

CHAPTER 7: **PRAY IN THE NIGHT**

I HAD scarcely left my yard heading for prayer down in the thickets one morning when I felt a strong urge to go back into my crib to call some friends who would accompany me to the session.

Taking a swift turn, I skated into the house and collapsed into my favourite chair as I yelled for my son to bring my phone.

Suddenly, before my eyes, I saw a small flicker of light which I thought to be the rays of the sun permeating my room, but the light grew rapidly possibly at the speed of thought.

I swept my eyes across the room as I stood to investigate this phenomena, but more drama was already unfolding, forcing me to go back to my chair, only frozen and awe-stricken this time.

I saw a humongous hand that suspended in the air moving towards my western wall. The forefinger unclenched and a tremor shook the house when it hit the granite tiled end. Like a chisel in its master's hand, the finger engraved words that remain dear to me. A voice that echoed as if from an empty arena followed:

"Pray in the night and hustle during the day!"

As I wondered at this prescribed cure to poverty, I found myself at the centre of a very huge arena, but the sun was atop inside it signifying that it was day-time.

It seemed to me that every race and nationality was here represented from time immemorial. People in the terraces held different instruments of work, mattocks, shovels and hoes, and dust littered the entire space as evidence that these folks were workers.

A banner in the rear top end of the arena uncoiled earthwards, I turned to see this spectacle and it read: "Work whilst it is day, the night comes when no man can work."

My amazement deepened as I gulped volumes of saliva to clear the dust from the arena that had settled on my throat.

A man on my side elbowed me, put his hand around my neck and took me out. We slid into the centre of another theatre relatively bigger than the previous one.

Again the sun was atop inside it signifying that it was day-time with every race and nationality represented in the terraces from time immemorial.

Most of the people were praying and answers were raining into the previous arena. I watched in utter grief as these religious folks missed the golden opportunities they had provoked from the heavens.

The man showed me the source of poverty for many in this world. He said they pray when they should be working and they sleep when they should be praying.

God blesses the work of our hands, not the prayers of our lips. Your devotion to the prayer room provokes solutions and your presence in the marketplace qualifies you to receive those solutions into physical reality!

Answers are experienced in the marketplace not in the prayer–mountain. Passionately, he looked at me as if he would spew fire from his mouth and cautioned:

"Pray in the night and hustle during the day."

He handed me four golden gifts of the night which he admonished me to share with the world. He said anyone who embraces these golden gifts sets himself for a glorious hustle in the marketplace.

- Pause
- Ponder
- Pray
- Plan

Pausing is rest which allows you to revive from the exhaustion of your previous hustle, pondering is meditation which makes you realise the depth, height and breadth of the potential you habour inside.

Prayer connects you to your source of livelihood and power. Finally, planning directs that life and power into everything that you do.

Pray in the night and hustle during the day!

CHAPTER 8: **STUDY MONEY**

YEARLY, governments spend a fortune on academics, the financially spruced send their children to expensive institutions available, and the poor also put aside from the little they eke just to afford their children an education.

Classes are filled with people who intend to get themselves knowledgeable in certain areas of specialty, but only a handful of people across the world take time to study money and understand it.

This way, we become masters of everything else except money! It is a good thing to know your job very well and a better thing to have the knowledge of money, however, the best thing is to have the knowledge of both.

Bus wheels reeled underneath me one summer evening when I dosed off in tiredness from a hard day that I had spent at the border. It was now twilight as the sky had begun to rot, the distant rays of the sun brushing-off their fading colour on the eastern Kalahari peaks paving way for dusk.

We had barely entered southern Africa's cowboy capital Gaborone when the roof of the vehicle slit-open before my eyes and, in no time, an elegant and glistening white eagle hovered the lower sky then stirred his wings taking a downward direction.

He unleashed his claws from the belly feathers like a plane does its wheels before hitting the runway.

He sunk his claws in both of my shoulders and snatched me out of the ride, separating my spirit from the body. In the distant, I remember seeing my body wasting on the seat as we glided the western trade winds.

We flew across the heat infested desert and hit ground on an oasis adorned with several springs of water and palm trees. A tent was pitched and a league of men, wearing an array of tuxedos, sat inside it. This indicated that the gathering was formal.

I spotted an empty seat then went over to occupy it. One of the elegantly dressed man walked over to the podium and the first words he uttered were:

"It is a good thing to know your job very well and a better thing to have financial knowledge, however, the best thing is to have an understanding of both."

I sat there pondering and figured that understanding your job very well gives you an advantage. You stand head and shoulders above your competition because cream always settles at the top. You mop a lot of clients and syphon great wealth, but without complete understanding, the liquid you mop from your hustle becomes a curse instead of a blessing. You end-up plaguing self with many troubles.

When I shook my head to re-integrate with the on-going presentation, the man was already re-affirming;

"It is a good thing to know your job very well and a better thing to have the knowledge of money, however, the best thing is to have an understanding of both."

"What is money then?" A question popped from the audience. At this moment, all my mental valves flung wide-open to suck every bit of —

knowledge the gurus would spit. I leaned forward like a colt pulling a heavy-cart uphill, with my elbow kissing my knee and right thumb caressing my small beard.

I expected to hear the answer from the facilitator of the gathering, but like a calf excited at seeing its mother, a pint-sized man who was sitting next to me leaped to tackle the question.

Listening to his wise words, I visualised how we often miss golden counsel from those who surround us, siblings, fellow workmates or those we worship with, simply because we seek for it in places and people far from our reach. I repented and resolved to glean financial wisdom first from sources that are primarily accessible to me.

"It is a good thing to be exceptional at your job and a better thing to have financial knowledge, however, the best thing is to have an understanding of both."

"Money is what it enables you to do for yourself and others, not necessarily the figures we have in the bank. It is an advantage you allow your future offspring, the smile you put on an orphan; the food you put on the table of an ailing granny; the education you allow the less privileged to have, the medication you afford the poor sickling or the good counsel you give to the stranded in life. No wonder the great teacher taught that it is more beneficial to give than to receive. Money is an object that gives us status, it amplifies our willingness to serve others," he said.

As I ruminated over these words of the wise one, my thoughts began speaking to me; I realised that the rich see needs as opportunities and in their quest to meet them, they better people's lives, but in the process, filling their chambers with gold and choice things this world offers.

Money is a currency, henceforth the wealth that gains eternal value for us is not necessarily that we hold or save to consume in our pleasure, but that which we put away for the pleasure of others, to hold and save our future generations and the needy in our day.

To afford myself a wider opportunity to fulfill this divine duty, I resolved to be smart at my job and even smarter at financial handling, lest that which I gain in my daily hustle turn and become a heap of dust that can be easily blown away by the winds of ignorance.

"It is a good thing to know your job very well and a better thing to have the knowledge of money, however, the best thing is to have –

an understanding of both."

My companion screamed in my ears, informing me that we had arrived at our destination, but I had a bigger lesson to celebrate. The Eight Laws of money had been added to my mental quiver.

- Be the best at what you do
- Grow your customer network daily
- Keep your customers like gold
- Acquire financial knowledge
- Accumulate financial value daily
- Reward yourself
- Invest for your future generations
- Help the needy

CHAPTER 9: **BE DISRUPTIVE**

THE MARKETPLACE is a deadly war zone and the captains of industry are the commanders in the battlefront. They accumulate great wealth because they suffer the most heat.

It's a myth to find a rich person with no problems, their secret lies in transforming their scars into stars. Hustling is like a furnace infested with intense heat of gruesome competition.

You need to continuously think on how to tackle challenges that seem impossible because any wink of slumber may lead to expiry.

It then requires the dexterities of survival to lead a profitable business life for a long time.

It was Christmas time when we went down to the village for a family reunion. We travelled through the dark and arrived home at the peak of the night, then normal as it is, everyone went straight to bed in preparation for the big reunion day.

I was exhausted from long travel, but my body was so nervous that I couldn't easily wade into sleep.

A little time elapsed, and when the homestead had gone totally silent, I heard a knock on the door, at first I was reluctant to attend to it then I rolled over to nap on my other side, before burying my head under a grave of blankets.

The knock roared again just like before, but the amazing thing was that I heard it the same way as before as if my head was still on the open.

I tried to wake my brother who shared the same bed with me, but he had already travelled far into the depths of slumber.

Reluctantly, I slid out of the blankets and paced towards the door. I stretched my arm to open it, but I went through it as if through the air. I leaked through the door and my next step stumbled me into the open yard. A vehement torrent surged from the nostrils of the wind scooping my feet off the surface.

I soared against gravity, and in an instant, landed on crystal-like platform decked with several multi-coloured rubies.

A table that seemed to be a mixture of gold and glass stood at the centre of this stage as the intricate nerves of lightning streaked all around it.

A voice boomed from the whistling wind, commanding me to collect a note from the golden bowl that sat at the centre of the table. I started for the table, but I seemed –

not to be arriving, I wasted in long and tiresome strides. At my point of exhaustion, the same voice thundered: "Life is a challenge, you need strength to achieve your goals, but strength alone isn't enough if you are to make the most from your hustle in the marketplace."

He continued: "Will power and determination of mind is the malt and sorghum that brews in you the audacity to win big."

I crawled on the quartzite floor with a renewed determination to reach for the note on the table and my instructor resumed his charge: "You are here to collect mental –

rudiments necessary for you to dominate the marketplace." At that point the note in the golden bowl formed in my hands and there was a written message with lessons that forge principals in the world of business."

• Be an Early Thinker
Ideas are a fruit of meditation. Timing of thinking determines the quality of thoughts that gravitate towards you. Reserve the early hours of the day for this cause. The probability to garner witty ideas is highest when your mind is fresh in the morning.

• Be a Creative Thinker
Train your mind to think creatively on strategies to implement your thoughts. Creativity determines the-

pace at which you takeover the market.

- Be a Disruptive Thinker

The marketplace is a jungle in which only the smart survive. Continuously build yourself and your business likewise with inventive thoughts and actions that outsmart your competitors.

Maintain a close eye on your competition and trends in business to avoid dismissal because they too have their eyes on you. Disrupt or be disrupted!

- Be a Timeous Executor

Here is what separates the rich from the poor. No matter how good your plans are, they can become a heap of dust if they are not executed accordingly.

To maximise profits, a wise farmer does not wait for rain in order to plant, but creates a conducive environment favourable for his crops to produce even when it's not their season.

Plans are most profitable when everyone thinks it's not their season, however, create a conducive atmosphere for their breeding before execution. The Bible teaches us to be instant in season and out of season.

CHAPTER 10: **MAXIMISE SELF**

I DREADED to wake up my wife earlier than she had planned, so, instead of switching on the light, I groped in the early morning darkness. I pulled my phone out from the charger to check the time, it was 0330am.

I was already thirty minutes late for my early morning mental drill. Quickly, I packed out of the bedroom and headed for my study.

Upon entering our sitting room area, I noticed a man who looked like me, a more perfected version of me though, sitting on my chair. He motioned his hand, inviting me to sit right next to him.

I wanted to freak out, but suddenly, an ether of God's love saturated my physicality, draining away all the fear.

I paced towards him and then co-alesced my hind before descending into the available space right next to him.

He handed me a pen and paper as he introduced himself. Then he told me that he was a messenger who had come to help me with my mental drill that morning.

He reminded me of a fable that my wise mother often reiterated to me during my high-school days, but he spoke of it in a more dramatic and inspiring way.

"Once there was a young man who was born and raised in a poor rural home. His colleagues at school with parents who could afford holidays in big cities often came back with loads of stories to share after each school break to which he would listen attentively, gulping each morsel of their experiences into the bowels of his soul. This birthed a dream within him to live in a big city some day.

One day, he bid his family goodbye and embarked on a journey that would take many days. On the way, he met an elderly man whom he befriended as they headed for the same city. Because they couldn't keep the same pace, the old man thought it good to capitalise on the strength of this young man. He trusted the young man with his money and instructed him to invest in the stock market upon arriving into the city.

He did this trusting that upon his arrival the money may have matured, leveraging him to conclude his days on earth in peace with no financial struggle.

Entering the big city was like a fairytale to this young man. The lights, glitz, music and beautiful girls lured him into club life to which he blew all the money that he had been trusted with.

After many days the old man finally arrived famished from long walk,
and was severely distressed when he
found out that the young man had
blown the money, instead of in-
vesting it. During his last days, the
old man lived from handouts and
finally died in poverty."

I kept looking at his graceful lips as
I guzzled saliva down my throat as a
gesture of understanding.

Then he said in jest: "There is an
old man or woman in every young
person you see roaming the streets.
Through wisdom he sends out a
young person in him first to prepare
a good life so that when he finally

arrives, he won't have to hustle for sustainability, but eat from the orchard the young person planted before him.

There are things we should utilise when we are young because they deplete as we age. They are the capital that every young person requires, use them and become great. In the end, your life will be celebrated when others are regretted."

These words sent chills down my spine, and I moaned on my seat, but I still wanted to hear more. He pat me on the shoulder and told me to write the following:

- Opportunities

When you embrace opportunities around you early in life, you will be in power the rest of your life.

Lack of qualification for a particular opportunity may delay you, but it will never hinder you from utilising other opportunities.

Opportunities produce the most for us when we are still young. One of them is the physical strength you have, it depreciates as you grow.

- Talent/Skills and Ability

Every person has a natural ability which God gave them to be sustained and empowered through it.

Discover the natural skills you possess as a young person and earn riches for a long time through utilising them.

• Ideas

These are like well water, the one who draws first, draws the freshest. When your mind honours you with an idea, act on it because in most cases it is your key out of a quagmire. It is another way to capitalise yourself.

• Money

This should be the least of our concerns when it comes to capital. Make use of the above three and money will follow.

Often money is the fruit of imple-
mented ideas, deployed talent and
exploited opportunities. Getting it
at the outset is a myth.

CHAPTER 11: **INVENT THE FUTURE**

BEING born into the planet earth should come with an undeniable expectation that bad things will happen. Factors that will make you cry or sometimes hate why you were born will be inevitable even to good people.

During such precarious moments, some whine as they brand themselves victims of bad omen and monopolies of misfortune, relegating the greatest life-transforming asset they have in possession — the human mind to wishing and begging.

Many times only a few make a robust resolve to be inspired by their misfortunes and inspire positivity and invoke a sense of worth into others around them.

We should come to a realisation that, in most cases, good things follow hard times because hardship is the ointment that nourishes our eyes to see and appreciate the good around us.

An understanding that hardship is the raw material of all progress should be coined within us.

Such a mental perspective will inspire you never to throw in the towel, but capitalise on situations that are against you, using them for own advantage.

You will glean the dexterity of survival and winning through experiencing adversity. Hardship is a tool that God uses to squeeze potential out of us.

Calmness is a myth most fools wait for. They wait for a time when resources are allowing to get an education, start a business or reach out to achieve certain life objectives. They wait for things to happen, instead of them happening to things.

Acquire a realisation that the only person and resource you have in control is chiefly you; things will not happen until you make them to happen.

Stop whining about this being not the best time to venture out while doing nothing in the interim.

This mental slothfulness will make you the living dead or a moving grave. You will be synonymous with the dead in more ways except one — the breath in your nostrils.

Be a doer, intoxicate yourself in action until it becomes natural just like breathing is to you — you don't put effort to do it.

Mental drudgery can cause you to wait for eternity, continue the rat-race of mediocrity and pass it on to the next generation.

Eagles glide the highest altitudes during storms. The best way to start is to start, you can never become until you begin.

An ancient orator bellowed: "He who observes the wind will not sow, And he who regards the clouds will not reap."

You can plant during drought and reap a hundred-fold. Venture out, set objectives for yourself, but not limits, the word "impossible" itself can be read: "I'm possible."

It sounds good this way as it inspires you to reach further. Engage people of different classes and widen your prospects.

The best time is now and now is the only time you have, maximise it. Approach life with an open mind and open heart.

Life is happening now, it's your duty to make things happen, don't wait for tomorrow for tomorrow may never come.

Do not leave for tomorrow what can be done today. Stop looking for resources to use in life, your life is the biggest resource, make use of it! Some opportunities only come once in a lifetime, chief of those is the very life you live. You can either make Progress or Excuses, but if truth be told; you can never make both at the same time.

You pass through this life once. Any good you can do, or any kindness you can show, do it now, do not defer or neglect it. For you shall never pass this way again.

Make a resolution to make everyday count, function in your purpose and dominate through it. Refuse to expire in potential, don't park in the now and expire in adversities.

Use hardship as a stairway to greatness, rob the grave of your potential and make a choice to die empty, having explored your potential to the fullest. You alone can make it illegal to die with dreams; no one else will make that decision for you.

Collaborate with your dreams and invent the future.

CHAPTER 12: **UP YOUR VOLUME**

The breath you are taking right now is a possible passport to the next one and it is sign that you are still alive — no matter how battered you feel.

It is showing you that you still have all the credentials of this life in one place, no matter how clumsy things around you are, and it is evidence that you still have a purpose to fulfill and an assignment to accomplish, no matter how disintegrated and disdainful you feel about yourself.

You are not yet done in this life as long as you can still see, feel, smell, taste or hear. Even if you are on your sickbed, you are livelier than a purposeless stray roaming the streets aimlessly, as long as you have a flicker of hope to see the next second within you. Keep that lit because it is the visa to your passport of breath.

With hope you can explore diverse lands of possibilities. Don't expire because of circumstances for your creator made you a master over everything that touches your life.

It is important to learn to embrace life wholesomely by planning for it and taking each day as a precious gift.

Treat every, second, minute or hour as an opportunity to express or activate your good plans and that will surely effect transformation in your life.

Learn from rain which floods the earth not because it falls from the sky as a river, but as droplets. Consistency is key!

You don't need to be a great person to accomplish great works. Great people are small men who decided to ace great assignments one bit at a time.

Plan and activate your plans daily lest you suffocate yourself by trying to execute everything at once. Don't wait until December to do everything you intended for the year — a year's plan can be broken into manageable and achievable quarterly, monthly, weekly, daily or even hourly missions.

Failingto plan is planning to fail and failing to act on those plans is passport to idleness and rottenness. Living with unapplied potential within you is worse than suicide.

It is a crime you will carry through eternity, living with regrets on this side of life and when you finally cross the curtain of time, your creator will ask for what you did with all that glorious deposit within you.

Failure to act on your plans is the ancestor of all poverty. Procrastination steals not only time, but who you should become — you park in a hoax and wait for a perfect day when everything permits you to act on your dream, but in the mean—

while depleting in your youthful vigour. Sadly, most people discover that such a day never arrives when they are old and wasted having massively depleted in both bodily and mental strength.

They conclude their days on earth in a nirvana, blaming their failures on other people. It is noble to credit other people with your successes when you always blame them for your failures.

The art of succeeding in life lies in starting early; an early bird captures the fattest worm. Start as soon as you come to the realisation that something ought to be done because the only time you have is now. Don't wait until tomorrow for that is not promised.

Don't let the sands of time run their course without making a vivid contribution in your life — and that of others.

The true value of life is gleaned from the seeds of positive contributions that we sow into others, not what we get from them.

Live your life like your best song, play it, turn up the volume of your mental gadgetry and dance through it like no one is watching.

Unpleasant circumstances may cross your path, but never allow them to steal your hope and joy for they are the fuel that keeps life rolling.

Stand-up to do the counting not to be counted anymore! Be in control and victimise your circumstances You're a created to be a master!

CHAPTER 13: **MAXIMISE HATERS**

IN THE world of sport, the objective of every athlete is to win. However, the plan to achieve this goal differs with the kind of discipline.

For racers on the tracks, this objective is achieved individually; thus the rider puts to the fore the best skill they have to vanquish fellow racers so they can lift the trophy.

The cliché, "Each man for himself, God for us all" is applied to its zenith in such disciplines. Whilst in other disciplines such as football or soccer the winning objective is most assured when each team–player contributes their best into the common pool called the Team.

Individualism is abhorred to the maximum as the beast-sized players chant; "united we stand; divided we fall!"

It is to the utmost truth that the people who collaborate well with others score better in life, reason being they capitalise on the strengths of others where they are weak.

They understand that strength in isolation is a weakness and weakness in another's company is strength.

They appreciate that strength and weakness are inseparable; the outcome of defeat or triumph is determined by the kind of people you choose to collaborate with.

Teams share responsibilities fairly amongst the participants, the idea of having someone watching your back makes the burden of loss easier to bear and the glory of winning sweeter to celebrate.

It is not weakness that makes people victims of defeat, weakness is an opportunity to capitalise on other peoples' strengths. It is a calling to go social.

Arrogance is the cancer gnawing the winning marrow of many, making their bone composition brittle, in the end, disfiguring their winning attributes to failure. Those who pretend to know it all and those who believe they are islands needing no one to —

make it will be snails in life. Speed and progress will remain foreign to them. To know is to be ignorant. Not to know is the beginning of wisdom.

The best things of life are a reward we get for combining our best efforts.

Winning is a goal we deliberately set for ourselves, lean towards it and work ourselves repeatedly towards achieving.

The movement of our bodies towards achieving it is, however, powered by the right attitude, for what is success other than a sound state of mind?

The best attitude views affliction as the oil of life; hence choosing to slide through it. Challenge your mental eyes to see all people as opportunities of destiny. People remain opportunities even if they oppose you; endure hardship, for it is triumphing over opposition that is ranked as a win.

Understand that history has less record of quitters; history is laden with encounters of people who believed that they wielded far better knowledge and dangerous instinct than any beast of the wild and thus drove themselves hard towards achieving what seemed myths in their day. Listening to stories of those who failed and never dared to stand again can weaken you. Launch out, sometimes the value of experience is overrated, usually by grey heads that nod wisely and speak stupidly.

Capitalise on the hell that your haters give you, combine their negative energy with your positive energy to power your locomotive of progress and the stones they throw at you into stepping stones to prosperity. This way they remain your companions of destiny.

Their actions should push you into vantages of a better life. This perspective will help you to turn your tears into pearls. Truth be told, you need enemies to make it in this life.

Affirm yourself because so long there is breath in you, you need to persist — if you persist long enough you will win. Allow your life to feed on negatives. The more the resistance, the more the oil you have to fatten self.

Winning is a hoax where there are no obstacles to overcome, keep pressing toward the mark for the high prize. Winning is the ultimate prize we get after continuous episodes of pressing and wiggling through obstacles.

Obstacles on your path are not there to impede your progress; they are there to inspire the best out of you.

The higher and tougher they are, the greater the resolve and determination to awaken the wildest instincts within. No resistance can stand for long before a man of determination and strategy, because the longer it stands, the more inspired he gets.

Don't expire because of obstacles in your path, rather be inspired to grow! Obstacles are an opportunity to grow, it's impossible to win gold without hurting. To win gold, you have be bold!

Challenges of life impart the realisation that we need the contribution of others to make it. Such thoughts are rare unless we encounter obstacles.

CHAPTER 14: **DEFINE YOURSELF**

IN ONE of his poetic songs, the village preacher quipped: "Why is the word dictionary in the dictionary?" Then he went on; "Is it because no one has the right to define others without he himself being defined?"

If life was a song, then I would describe these words as the chorus, reason being they are words worth repeating generation after another. They are pregnant and timeless!

The prophecy of our future is dependent on how we respond to our circumstances and the true definition of self is extracted from the pollens of personal experience.

It is from overcoming those tempestuous episodes of life that we obtain a sense of worth. We should gear ourselves with a mentality and attitude that doesn't shudder in the face of a fire-arrayed furnace.

The reward we should look ahead to obtain out of every heated test of life are the lessons which help us to become high-voltage leaders across all scopes of life. Crisis is a terrible thing to waste.

There is always something good to obtain out of every crisis. Crisis is the first half of a match called opportunity; you will not enjoy the pleasure in the second half when you evade learning from adversity.

Learning from crisis precedes all meaningful and lasting pleasure of life. Your adversities should refine you to become the best you were created to be in all facets of your life.

Aim to be a better team player as a wife or husband, an adorned executive or employee by taking daily steps of progress towards obtaining a particular goal in life.

Don't throw in the towel when the furnace throws a hot wind in your face, heroes are not born heroes, they are made through remaining positive when its not fashionable to do so. Speaking of Jesus; a first century writer to the Hebrews asserted:

"...who for the joy that was set before Him endured the cross, despising the shame..."

We can stir our resolve to remain on course towards achieving greatness when we have the audacity to despise the shame of this present moment, the shame of starting small or the shame to forego the delicacies of youthful desires choosing to invest for the future instead.

A wise elder once told of his married daughter who visited with a list of complains on how life was mistreating her. As she grieved, she motioned to make a point. With a deep sigh, she rolled off to describe her misfortunes in remarkable celerity:

"My husband… my boss… my friends… are making me miserable. I am having a tough time dad." For ninety minutes, the father listened attentively, until she finally came to a halt.

The old man didn't say a word, but instead strode to the kitchen which stood directly opposite his sitting room.

He took an egg and swum it into the water then brought it to boil, when it was ready, he spooned it out and sat it in a plate. He took a few carrots, chipped them and threw them into a pot, poured water which he boiled as well. When they got ready he poured them in the same plate.

Lastly he grabbed a few coffee beans in his palm, filled the same pot with water and streamed them in, made them to boil then he poured the water into the cup.

The father gently asked her daughter to feel the carrots in the plate. She did and observed the carrots had gone soft and could easily crush them between her fingers. He asked again to feel the egg. This time she did, but with little reluctance, the observation was that the egg had gone hard. The father finally asked her to smell the coffee then sip it.

She glowed as the tantalising aroma billowed through her nostrils. It tasted good.

"It tastes delicious and refreshing dad" she said.

"I subjected all these three under the same condition, but we got three different outcomes. The egg is hardened, the carrot has gone soft and the coffee bean changed, but a little, however, it changed the water to coffee and made it to taste good," he rumbled.

Then with his booming voice he continued: "Choose to become an egg and you will become callous, you will develop a cocoon and become a social misfit. Your adversity would have made a terrible person to relate with. Choose to become a carrot and you will be taken advantage of.

Growing weak in the face of adversity is a sure sign that you never had inner strength. This way you will live at the mercy of other people.

However, if you decide to become a coffee bean, your adversity will inspire you to change your surroundings and you will become better after every test. You will be lovable and make friends; you will stand to benefit a lot in life."

We must not give hardship the credit of burying people's potential. Don't be a victim in life, allow your circumstances to sculpt you into the best person you dream of becoming.

CHAPTER 15: **OBTAIN GLORY**

"**YOU PREPARE** a table before me in the presence of my enemies" is a common line in the Hebraic literature with its ancestral origins from the mouth of King David.

These words have transcended the tables of time and have sired remarkable testimonies of greatness in the history of humanity across the entire human race on all platforms.

This is so because of the inspiration behind the words, they pump energy and audacity to overcome adversity and achieve greatness in the heart of the reader. They are the kind that impute a mental eye that spots opportunity during moments of severe crisis and compel the host to commit to action, obtain a name and hog glory in the timeline of history.

This psalm stirs an insatiable hunger in the guts of imagination, bringing with itself a formidable understanding that history can only be made if we are deliberate with making it.

Greatness can only be nurtured through adversity and it is when we triumph over resistance that we are tagged history-makers.

It emboldens this reality in our souls; hardship happens to everyone, it's our response to it that shape our destiny. This way we choose to become the best out of our suffering.

We join the band wagon of greatness that has its confluence at the horizons of both the living and the dead understanding that adversity without triumph isn't inspiring.

By following what it prescribes, we immortalise ourselves. We start ripples of grapevine that will, in the process of time, turn to waves of influence. Generations that emerge after us will echo our writings, poems, songs and names. They will recite them as long as humans will live.

Today, the world speaks of ordinary people who understood that they were created for an extra-ordinary purpose and took up the noble cause to challenge their limits. People like Mahatma Gandhi and Nelson Mandela chose to be concerned with national issues when they should have taken a back seat.

Albert Einstein was inspired by a Chinese proverb: "It is better to light a candle than to curse the darkness" and thus was led to invent a light bulb, my black brother, George Washington Carver was inspired by a cotton weevil that had destroyed the hope of the poor peasants, convinced them to grow peanuts and went on to discover hundreds of products that a mere peanut would produce. Among the discoveries were cosmetics, oils and stock feeds. From his laboratory, Carver managed to inspire industrialists to-produce the products he had discovered.

Martin Luther became a revivalist when it was revealed to him that justification is by faith not by works and thus was used to pioneer a vibrant and lively way of worshiping. However, he risked losing his life at the hands of radical Catholic monks of his time.

What made these people extra-ordinary was not in their phenomenal births or peculiar upbringings, but it was the realisation that there is no table of choice food that can be arrayed before us without triumphing over adversity. Enemies are an opportunity for glory, the secret to —

overcome them is harboured in the vaults of learning.

Learning prepares us for the opportunities ahead and by the time an opportunity called enemy pops up before us, it will be too late to prepare.

Develop yourself every opportunity you find. Forbid the sun to go down into the western horizon without making an addition to your worth.

Paul of Tarsus was on the spot when he penned this timeless advice to his young mentee Timothy: "Study to shew thyself approved unto God, a workman that cannot be ashamed…"

History doesn't discriminate people — it can be made by anyone despite their age, background or class. The choice to make it remains personal; you cannot delegate it to another!

CHAPTER 16: **BE TEACHABLE**

"**WISDOM** is the reward you get for a lifetime of listening when you would have preferred to talk." These gut-churning words of columnist Doug Larson were recently re-conveyed into my soul when I came across this aggravating story.

It is barely a month after a thirty-five-year-old single mother had bought her first brand-new Mercedes and was so obsessed with it to an extent that she neglected to share personal moments with her six-year-old son in the days that followed, moments her little sunny boy was accustomed to and so dearly cherished. The boy tried to reach out to her mum and inform her how desperately he —

missed the nights they would cud-
dle and watch cartoons together as
well as popcorn weekends. "Hon-
estly mum I miss your love . . . and
I am tired of your forehead kisses."
He protested.

One fine Saturday morning, the
mother was busy doing laundry in
the bathtub when the boy strayed
to the back of the house where he
picked himself a sharp-edged stone
and began to excavate through the
mud. In his mind he saw himself
chatting a huge truck through the
cross-border highway.

When he finally got to the front of
the house he saw the new car parked
and thought to convey a message to

his mother that said: "I love you mum and I miss you." However, this time around, instead of darting into the house to tell his mother, he simply paced towards her mother's new navy blue toy where he decided to convert his cross border truck into a writing instrument.

At around the same time the mother was now lining her washing outside the house, she heard some tiny screeching noises. She strode to the front of the house and saw the entire bonnet scratched in gibberish and her boy standing besides the car holding his sharp-edged stone. The mother's anger mounted and she picked a hard electric cable and started beating her son.

The moment she felt her anger was satiated, she opened her eyes to a debilitating sight.

The boy was severely injured and was by this time unconscious. The rest is history, but the boy suffered life time injuries; a broken rib and broken fingers. When she left the child writhing on a hospital bed to bring some supplies from the car, she took time to understand the scratch on the car. It read exactly what her little son had tried to speak to her: "Mum I love you and I miss you."

To most people talking comes more natural than listening. They hate listening because subconsciously it's ingrained within them to believe —

that people around will take that for a weakness. Even during discussions, some people only listen to answer back, impeding the actual object of listening. We should listen to learn.

When you listen with the spirit of learning, you ignite a teachable spirit within you and with the very same rock you thwart the spirit of pride.

Pride impedes hearing in the end it cripples understanding. A man who gives himself to it is foolish and shallow and makes it impossible for him to learn anything new.

Most help comes to such people once, but because they treat it with contempt, it never returns to them.

Help comes to those who embrace it! If experience is the best teacher, then choose to learn from other people's experiences — this way you wax greater in a short space of time by avoiding the traps and pits that other people experienced.

Had the mother in the narrated story listened to her son in time by keeping her priorities in line, she would have avoided the physical and emotional injury she caused her son.

Had she sought to understand the meaning of the scratch on the bonnet, she would have gotten the love message from reading it and a chance to repent before causing such grievous harm.

Mostly, we realise that the opportunities of learning are gone past us when we are in danger, but how foolish we become when we let such reminders vapour from our spirits.

Treat every person you encounter as having something to teach you and when you wake up to a new day— embrace it as an opportunity to learn.
Learning prepares us for the opportunities ahead and it is impossible to learn without cultivating the virtue of listening.

Learning associates with all greatness just as all mental smallness is fueled by "I know it all" attitude.

Attitude is a choice, so is teachability. We can choose the pathway to a better future or life by developing a teachable spirit, or we can sabotage that future by pretending that we know everything required to figure it out in this life.

No one subject or set of subjects will serve you for a foreseeable future, let alone the rest of your life. Maximising your potential in life requires extensive acumen which only comes through the learning portal.

Greatness is not a one man job, you need the contribution of others to be successful and that only comes through teachability

CHAPTER 17: **YOU'RE A SUPERSTAR**

IT IS mid–August in the year of 1997 and the winds are blowing vehemently, the trees are swaying back and forth in the gust of incessant whirlwinds.

I am pacing down the cattle trail in the midst of a savanna plain when through the semi-thick haze of dust, I recognise an approaching strange figure that seemed burdened.

As it drew nigh, I noticed an ailing old man, perhaps in his eighties, wheezing like a yoked donkey, hobbling and staggering in the gust with vivid traces of sweat littering his entire brow, having been blown away in the direction of the wind.

He had what seemed a satchel on his back, with the bottom area of it sticking out with what seemed like lumps, making it obvious to me that this octogenarian was carrying something heavy for his old-spin-dly-body.

This whole picture demand-ed that I give a hand to this old hobbler. "Hey old-timer, can I carry that for you?" He slowly halt-ed and turned to me with a somber look, the roll in his eyes signaled that he needed the help.

I reached out to unburden him of his satchel, then I realised it was heavier than I thought. "What's in the bag grandpa?" I quizzed.

Of cause I was astounded with the reply that followed. "They are stones my son." He quivered from exhaustion.

He then continued: "I received good news, my daughter who has been struggling to have a child for fifteen years has given birth to a boy and I am going to share all my joy with her".

"I stay in the village across the plain so to make sure that I would reach my destination without being blown away by the wind, I resolved to carry a few rocks in my bag so I may gain a more solid and heavier stamina against it".

I marveled at how this old hobbler had thought about re-inventing his youthful vigour that could cause him to trot across plains unrestrained by countering vehement forces like wind.

He believed not only in the beauty of his dream but he believed also in seeing and cherishing it. No force can withstand a dream whose time has come. William Arthur Ward was right when he indited these timeless words: "If you can imagine it, you can create it. If you dream it, you can become it."

The old man had already walked the journey in his mind and had overcome the tempest on the way by the power of positive thought. He had already seen his grandson in his imagination, which is why he took the calculated risk and launched into the deep.

Help met him on the way not in his hut. In the first century biblical passage, it is recorded that the ten lepers commanded by Jesus to go and present themselves to the priest were healed as they went. Grab your coat and say goodbye to demeaning factors around you then leave for your place of assignment which is purpose.

You will realise that the best experiences of life are not waiting at the destination but along the path of —

your quest for purpose. As you ped-
dle on, you will be associated with
growth, fulfillment and wealth. You
can never become until you begin.

You can never cross the ocean unless
you have the courage to lose sight of
the shore and the desire to experience the deep. You too can mimic
this old but wise way, pack your bag
of life with various stones in the form
of mentors, positive friends, family,
education and the list goes on.

These solidify you during times
when tempests are on rampage.
Capitalise on your strength and make
it so vivid that your weakness ob-
scures in the gleam of it. Feed your
strength every moment you find

through positivity, self discipline, good association, education or accountability. You starve your weakness to death not by focusing on how it's impeding your progress, but by keeping your mind on what makes you strong.

Factor this out and you will glide on the wings of greatness. We are all born superstars, however, the difference lies in our determination to pull that gem out of us.

History is awash with persons that were giants on the inside not necessarily on the outside, people who made a resolution to pull-out the giants within. Winning is in the venom of the dynamite within you, not your outward size. Little David slayed a six-foot tall Goliath and a stout Napoleon overran almost the whole of Europe. The mighty Goliaths of life tumble before us if we capture such a fiery disposition — an attitude of Faith in Action!

Thank you for taking
interest in reading
The God's Hustler. I trust you
have been nourished greatly
and you are now
set to dominate in life
and the marketplace.

For feedback, Sales and
Bookings please contact
our office on:
+263774357394
+263719357394
hello@libertykingsdale.org

NOTES

www.ingramcontent.com/pod-product-compliance
Lightning Source LLC
Chambersburg PA
CBHW021411210526
45463CB00001B/317